Composition Studies

poems by

Annie Hinkle

Finishing Line Press
Georgetown, Kentucky

Composition Studies

Copyright © 2016 by Annie Hinkle
ISBN 978-1-63534-053-2 First Edition
All rights reserved under International and Pan-American Copyright Conventions.
No part of this book may be reproduced in any manner whatsoever without written permission from the publisher, except in the case of brief quotations embodied in critical articles and reviews.

ACKNOWLEDGMENTS

A slightly different version of "Dear writer" was published as "Ohio Summer" in *Ascent*, Volume 23, Number 3, Spring 1999.
"artists' agreement" was published in *Best of Ohio 2014*, Ohio Poetry Day Awards.
"museum tour" received National Runner-Up in the 2014 Cultural Center of Cape Cod Poetry Contest, judged by George Bilgere.
"writing lesson in silver" was published as "Writing Lesson" in *Southern Poetry Review*, Volume 52, Issue 2, 2014.

I am grateful to many inspirational and supportive community members in The Greater Cincinnati Writers League, Cincinnati Writers Project, The Creative Writing Vision Program at Thomas More College, and The Practice of Poetry with Pauletta Hansel.

Publisher: Leah Maines

Editor: Christen Kincaid

Cover Art: "Apple Series" oil on paper. Richard Cisneros

Author Photo: Kira Ann Hinkle

Cover Design: Elizabeth Maines

Printed in the USA on acid-free paper.
Order online: www.finishinglinepress.com
also available on amazon.com

Author inquiries and mail orders:
Finishing Line Press
P. O. Box 1626
Georgetown, Kentucky 40324
U. S. A.

Table of Contents

Prologue 1

Dear Writer 2

poesia per musica 3

buried treasure 4

this poet 6

read me 7

artists' agreement 8

art lesson one 9

art lesson two 10

museum tour 11

city public 13

between writers 15

forgive me 17

writing in the garden 18

in memorium 20

autumn memory 21

snow 22

writing lesson in silver 24

Epilogue 26

For Steve

*Through the night
the apples
outside my window
one by one let go*

From "Falling: The Code" by Li-Young Lee

Prologue

I read your book

as one long sentence
ignoring
time
hunger
ache
in this way
pears
on page 6
became more related
to the *sun*
on 20
once
when I turned
the page
pearl
touched
light.

Dear writer

invite me to your porch
in the country
on your swing
we can talk about the moon
look at the light
falling
onto fields of Silverqueen
acres of soy

sing to me

dear writer
let me stay long enough
to see the corn ripen
into pearls
the green plowed
back to earth
while every night
fireflies become stars
Braille for my heart

dance with me

dear writer
please help me remember
that it is topography
I love
that landscape
leads to poetry
and this I would have
with you
on your porch
in the country

hold me there

poesia per musica

you share a partbook in progress
only one
of six melodies
in your new madrigal
the softness of your flute
whispered breath
fingertips on silver
and I try to hold
the line of notes
while imagining other parts
I heard yesterday
weaving around this sound
that comes from deep within
your 21st century
Renaissance mind

between notes
we are in Italy
where you will read original prints
and pore over parchment
that makes you weep
while I study stars
in the domes nearby
because I am looking for the perfect word
for line seven of this poem

we walk in the Apennines
through pines and firs
over smooth mounds of Carrara marble
layered under the forest floor
where we find a place
for an evening rest
a toast

to music and words
not yet composed

buried treasure

every birthday
my grandmother
gave me a book
      never stories
      never poems
but treasured collections
about the sky
the earth
and sea
volumes of stars
flowers
shells

I kept my favorite pages
open on my desk
under the lamp
sometimes
Domesticated Mammals
explanations and pictures
of rabbits
guinea pigs
dogs
and cats
as if to say
without speaking
to those
in and out of my room
how much I wanted
a pet

sometimes *Reptiles*
coiled and patterned
I'd dare myself
to touch them
Water Moccasin
Cobra
King

and once
after reading Robert Frost
in school
I noticed an arrow on page 115
pointing near Ohio
marking blueberries
on the *Origins of Fruit*
world map

but I already knew
blueberries were "ebony skinned
the [blue] but a breath
from the mist of the wind"

Frost, Robert. "Blueberries." *The Poetry of Robert Frost.* Ed. Edward Connery Lathem. New York: Holt, Rinehart and Winston. 1969.

this poet

is taking painting classes
in order to perfect the lesson
all meaning in things

> moon sea
> sun snow
>
> windows
> rooftops
> doors
>
> pears
> poppies
> pearl earrings
>
> draped silk
> porcelain skin
> folded hands
>
> eyes

deserve more than words

I mix blues and greens
on wax paper
while looking at the canvas
white taut
and waiting
for my heart now glazed
in color

read me

my silvered hair
on fire with moonlight
my eyes
weeping words
my breasts
dripping ink

yesterday my tongue
was purple
because I held a plum
my legs liquid
because I imagined the banks
of the Arno

artists' agreement

I caught you
not looking

I was in the café
you walked right by

didn't we promise

to keep our eyes open
for the sake of art

but you didn't see

the woman wearing feather earrings
bread just out of the oven
yellow chairs the color of your socks
I love
the glaze on the strawberry tarts
the waiter wiping his brow with white linen
gold lettering on the window

by my table

art lesson one

I couldn't take it anymore
so I bought a red dress
the color of my painting
fire at age six
even though my teacher said
flames weren't red
but what did she know
about the color
of heat
lips
apples
hearts
blood
she did not stop me
from painting
or writing
and I am certain
it's exactly the right color
made from linen
lined in silk
long
painted on

art lesson two

I put the apple in the last poem
for you
I remembered when you told me
about the day a man
happened to bite into one
at the precise moment
you were walking ahead of him
      the red sheen
      breaking
      echo of absence
and that you have been trying
for years
to write about this apple

passionately
of course

I put the apple there for you
a good spot in the stanza
central
so at the precise moment
of turning the page
it would happen to be there
in front of you
the apple
all over again

museum tour

I have seen *Water Lilies*
before
a panorama
in Washington, D. C.
in a white room
with windows
as big as canvases
the opening night
crowd
        black ties
        silk dresses
        champagne
        and raspberries
its own portrait of black white and burgundy
dots
before the blues and greens
across the room
Toulouse-Lautrec over Monet
in layers

I have seen them in Paris
with too many people
visiting
stuffy
noisy
and dim
I hurried to my picnic
        outside
        the blanket
        the basket
        treats from the shops
I closed my eyes
and only then
could see the lilies
properly

***

today
I am seeing them
again
in the midwest
where I first learned
about the relationship
of water
and sky
        summers at the pool
        eyeing clouds
        fearing storms
        and lightning
weather changing over water

all those years of light
revolving
rising up
again
and again
over this familiar land
where I grew
and aged
now

        here
        open
        floating

Monet, Claude. *Water Lilies*. 1914-1918. Oil on canvas. Musee de l'Orangerie, Paris.

city public

I sit outside the library
thinking I will not go in
this time
knowing
that if I open the door
to words
I will leave this earth
and evaporate
yet again
into flames
or frost

the residue of reading

exhausts me so
today I will stay
on this garden bench
grounded
with a view
of buses and taxis
vendors and cyclists
tourists jugglers and shoppers
before they are placed in lines
and still

the objects of writing

exhilarate me so
as the clarinetist
sitting
at the foot of the steps
still as a poem
but moving
blues
notes

letters
through the air

rising like a question

between writers

it has been 200,000 words
since I've seen you
do you know how many times
I've encountered the word *and*

counting what I've read
what I've written
(never mind what I've imagined)
approximately 5 times per page
2,340 pages

sometimes when I'm reading
a poem
a novel
or the screen of my computer
I cannot help but think

so much has happened in print

you always stopped
to buy the newspaper
after our talks
words over the table
between writers
"wait here" you'd say
"I'll just be a moment"
(one Mississippi, two Mississippi
I'd count like a girl)
and then you'd fold it
headline in half
and tuck it under your arm
words against words
saved for later

I hear the creasing
of your leather jacket
even now
a's
n's
d's
squeezed

at this moment
I am reading the paper

"A fresco—depicting what experts believe is a bird's eye view of how Rome looked before it burned down—has been discovered painted on a partly submerged wall. The fresco measuring approximately 10 ft by 6ft was found at the weekend on an ancient Roman wall on the Equiline Hill. Its size suggests that it may have served to remind Nero of how the city was before he let it burn down. It is bluish in overall tone, with buildings colored red. Temples are highlighted and..."

like most writers
I dream of words
falling into the right places
within sentences
noun—verb—object

EXPERT DISCOVERS FRESCO

man finds beauty

are you reading
are you writing
and

Johnston, Bruce. "The Rome of Nero is brought to light." *The Daily Telegraph*. 5 March, 1998: 12.

forgive me

for I have not read you today

I have brushed my hair
I have buttered toast

I have hand-washed stockings
I have polished old spoons

I have walked in the park
I have watched children play

I have sliced a lemon
I have sipped iced tea

I have paged through books
I have put them away

I have touched the window

writing in the garden

these poems need a paperweight
or they might fly away
like you
right out of my imagination
only weeks ago
just as the asters bloomed
near this table
where I am working

I place my coffee mug
on fluttering words
and remember
Aunt Ev's paperweights
how she flipped the switch
to light the glass shelves
for her narration
of the collection
rounds
ovals and squares
teardrops and hearts
dated and signed

"Do you want to hold one?"

I wanted to
slip my hand
in her pocket
get the key
and release
the criss-crossed rainbows
and peacocks
with gold and green swirled plumes
the swan with its beak
tucked into its neck feathers
the ring of blue butterflies

and the queen
especially the queen
stuck in her coronation robe
so high on the shelf
I had to look underneath
to see her

my heart is a red stone
my limbs are leaden
only my mind moves
like these poems
ready to fly
away

in memorium

when I finally face
the black and white truth
of you
I enlarge these poems
and glue them
on 2 by 3 canvases
work at my dining room table
a funeral banquet
a feast

I drop paint
from high above
like rain
bleed colors
into the tenor of the words
these vehicles
now empty

      no apples
      no moons
      no plums

on one canvas
I paint a new poem
in silver
take it to the garden
prop it between the trellis
and mums

angle it to catch the sun

autumn memory

at twelve
I leaned into the ladder
stretched my arms in an arc
beyond myself
under the green
umbrella of apples
the music of names
filling me

> *Rome Beauty*
> *Russet Empire*
> *Lady*

sisters and cousins
wagons and baskets
cider and honey

the best photo of that day
is of the ride home
sitting in the back seat
holding my favorite

> stem
> leaf
> shine

cupped in my hands
the tiny red globe

mine

snow

white
writing

writing lesson in silver

tonight
I'll leave the garden gate
open
the lights
off
you'll have to feel
your way
from gate
to wall
to window
to the ivy growing
alongside the kitchen door
which will be unlocked
though it sticks
sometimes
swollen
from October air
just push
and keep moving
into the room
where I will be waiting
in darkness
not for a kiss
but for you to describe
how it feels
coming to me
on fingertips
the wood
the stone
glass
and brittle vines
like bones
bracing themselves
for another season
of cold

and how it feels
especially
in the last moments
when you are completely alone
when there is nothing nearby
to touch
only faith
in the existence
of your words.

Epilogue

I read your book

twice
because the last
words
led me back
to the first
Dear
echo
hollow
white space
on each page
revealing
time
hunger
ache.

Annie Hinkle writes poetry, fiction, and picture books. Her work has appeared in *Ascent, Mid-American Review, Best of Ohio 2014, Express Cincinnati, Other Voices,* and *Southern Poetry Review,* and she has won a Walter Rumsey Marvin Grant, of the Ohioana awards, for fiction. She holds a B.A. from Xavier University; an M.A. in Creative Writing from Miami University where she was the founding editor of *Oxford Magazine*; and a Ph.D. from University of Kent, Canterbury, England. In addition, she has studied at Ropewalk, Chautauqua, Martha's Vineyard Institute of Creative Writing, and Breadloaf while teaching composition and creative writing at Miami University and University of Cincinnati. Currently, she teaches language arts and directs The Writing Center at Ursuline Academy in Cincinnati, Ohio. This is her first published poetry chapbook.

www.ingramcontent.com/pod-product-compliance
Lightning Source LLC
LaVergne TN
LVHW040117080426
835507LV00041B/1592